Out of Kilter
Poems: 1970-2020

by

Bernell MacDonald

Front cover by Stefan Keller

Books by Bernell MacDonald:

Poetry

I can really draw eagles
seeds we planted
)parentheses(
the theories of fish
in my own image
dog days
birds of passage
abiogeneses
Zoopoesies
poems in f minor
Wine River
Out of Kilter

Science

An Illustrated Miscellany of Animal Facts, Feats & Records

Fiction

The Monster of Moneymore
One Day the Animals Talked
The Moneymorians
Gypsy
The Black Wolf & Other Stories of the Old West
Collected Stories

MacDonald, Bernell, 1948-, author
    Out of Kilter / Bernell MacDonald.

ISBN 978-1-928020-20-2

Lion's Head Press
1820 Moneymore Road
Roslin, Ontario
KOK 2YO

CONTENTS

Dedicated to the memory of my friends:

Alden Nowlan, Fred Cogswell, Al Pittman,
Raymond Fraser, Ernest Buckler & Leo Ferrari

and for Marlene,
wherever you are

Out of Kilter

Poems: 1970-2020

Wine River

snapping photos of my
old haunts i can't believe
how the places have changed

fifty years ago
my girlfriend and i used to
make love in that old barn
but now the roof and walls are
caved in—the rafters and beams
broken and rotted

but despite the years
parts of the old stone foundation
still stand and
wherever you may be
darling
i just want you to know

you were always in the picture

two flights

a fledgling
bird
slammed into
my front door
window today
reminding me
of an incident
back in my
university days
when a girl on
acid
jumped out of
the seventh-story
dorm window
thinking
she could fly

déjà vu

spring and
a darkening day

i walk with the desire
to hope
but no beginnings here
and no ends

for it all seems
somehow familiar to me
the time
the place

it scares me
to think that I have travelled
this road before
that the experience relives itself

and my fear is heightened
by the sudden realization
that there may be no choice
in the way I choose to go

that i am living
my life in circles

and the circles
are getting smaller

spring, 1970 (Fredericton)

a spring night finds me in a cab

a drunken whore squeezes me
to tell if i am male or not

i slap her hands as i might
a naughty child's

impatiently
i wait to receive my change

sap rising in the trees

Ant

walking
down the sidewalk
this morning
I met an ant
who
was going
in the same direction
as Me
so I decided
to give him
until
the next crack
before
I stepped on him
i have also
sat
far into the night
wondering
Who
gives me time
to live for my own death

anthrophobia

i need provisions
  but people
    live in town

regardless
  i must leave
    the reclusion of
my farm and
  drive the distance

my nerves are shot

did you know
  the Mbuti nomads
    of the Congo
call village people
"savages"?

selves

i didn't mean
to hurt you darling

nor did i mean
to kick the dog

forgive me

i am a crowd

a thousand imposters
gather among me

the Urological Argument

standing
alone
miles from anywhere
in the middle
of a frozen lake
urinating
i have
the terrible
and awful feeling
that Somebody
is watching me

A man climbed a mountain

A man climbed a mountain
to seek wisdom from a sage

At the summit
he entered a cave and
accosted an old man
deep in thought

"Elder,
I am slashed by jagged stones—
torn by thorn—
breathless from this mountain's
thin air—"

"What mountain?"
replied the sage

old photograph

my mother
is not yet seventeen

is most beautifully smiling
in the afternoon sun; i tell you
that moment
will never cease being

her feet are stained
with red Island clay

her long wild hair
moves with the summer breeze

and in the trees, trees
too incredibly high
for any photograph

birds are singing

learning to fly

once
when the desire overflowed
i flew
it was a grand feeling
and i was happy
and prouder than hell

and there were those who watched

then...
i saw the birds
and fell suddenly
almost to my death

someday
i will fly again

and there will be no birds

the girl in a bikini

as i paddle the canoe
along the shore
lonely and depressed
head filled with
unwritable poems
a cottage girl in a bikini
suns herself

she is off a ways but i
can tell that she is young
and beautiful

i think she is reading a book—
a book of poems

she looks up from my book
and waves
for she is terribly in love with me

how could it be otherwise

first words over new grave

there!

ive planted your flowers
as requested

they look nice in the sun

their roots should take
despite the heat

ive watered them well
since there'll be no rain

i'll visit later
when the kids are in bed

and when theres no weather

the proselytizer

he tried so hard
  to make me believe
    in *his* version of the Bible

he forgot i was an atheist

haunted houses

as boys we created fear for sport
imagined headless men
moving through darkness
behind windows
—we dared strike
with stones through glass
dared kick the doors ajar

now though i am a grown man
i cannot stop the imagining—
glass in my windows
locks on my doors

horizons

a man lost on an endless desert
crawled towards the horizon
—suddenly
a speck of hope before him

but alas!

it was just a skeletal man
arms outstretched
grasping at his own
horizon

the light

lost in a dark
jungle
for years
a man prayed
to many gods
for deliverance
until one day
he saw a light
at the edge of the forest
and there a great plain—

—an endless plain devoid of trees

painting a robin

i am a poet
i write paintings for you

consider this robin:
notice
how i have his head
cocked for the worm

watch now!
watch!

look
how he flies
out of the canvas

into my painting

when you come to know a stranger

when you come to know a stranger
  as a friend or as a lover
    and then you separate
you will find that you have taken unto yourself
  that part of him in which you saw yourself
    reflected
and that he has taken unto himself
  that part he saw in you
    always
you will discover that part of you he took
  reflected in another
    so that what you took you kept
and what you lost you found

  this
    is how we slowly come to know ourselves

the closet monster

a shuffling woke me in the night
the monster was stirring in my closet

    but why was he turning the handle of the door?

i jumped out of bed
and ran downstairs screaming

my parents told me
to get back upstairs and to sleep

    that there was no such thing as monsters
    and nothing to be afraid of

    (but the one in my closet
    had always lived there)

and i could have sworn that i was scared

the old couple (for Art & Emmy)

i have to laugh
every time i visit
the old couple—friends
of mine:

somewhere in the middle
of a three-way conversation
old Art will conjure up
a disagreement—
issue a string of insults
at his wife
then turn and wink at me

then old Emmy in turn
will issue *her* insults right back
then turn and wink at me

after fifty years of marriage
—private people they are—
they still love each other enough
to want to display it
somehow in public

from the convent window

a nun
saw
the whole
thing
speeding car
bloody child
turned
quickly
clutched
her
crucifix
prayed
to God
because
she
couldnt
believe
it had
really
happened

this is mankind:

billions of people at the beach

some in the water
some out of the water

some laughing
some crying

some with faces
some without faces

billions of people at the beach
billions of little islands without shores

cutting wood in spring

spring and
  the circle
    finds me again

    treeless roots
  send forth
their sap

the skeptic

while hunting
we sighted
what appeared to me to be
nothing other than a Sasquatch
running into the denser bush

"Did you see it too" i managed
to ask in rhetorical question

"There's no such thing" my friend replied
"And besides, it looked like a fake to me"

epitaph

stranger,
too long have you stood
and stared at this old stone
with its buried bones

friend,
sit and rest your weary bones—
my stone is your stone
my bones are your bones

poem for afterlove (for Marlene)

i do not know
the things
       which drove me ungentle
nor
do i know the things
         which now
bloat me with regret

i know
only that you are gone
   and gone away

and i am sitting here too young
to be left this old

Carl

one day
i threw a bone to a dog

the next day he was back for rind and fat

the next for gravy and meat

an echo in the night

night
    fell
        all around me
and i
inching my way back
along
the swampy lakeshore
towards
my camp
        whistling
        and talking out loud
        my bribes to the night
startled
a loon into
flying
        up and over the lake
        and over the roof of the forest
        and then down
        down and into the last remnant
        of twilight
and in the distance
i heard him laugh

        and i laughed back

but O the loneliness
that rattled my soul

as the echo followed him

        followed him

the zoologist attends a baby shower

forced to attend
a baby shower
i find myself the only
male in a room
with ten women
who go on and on about
the darling and beautiful baby
while all i see before me
is the ugliest offspring
ever birthed by any species
in the animal class Mammalia

girl on crowded steps

i knew her wholly
at the instant
our eyes met

i loved her wholly
at a glimpse

when i spun round
she was gone, gone

this was twenty years ago
and only penned today

know then
why no man has loved greater
or suffered greater loss

on the pornography issue

why take the magazines
and videos off the shelves

why not start with the *real*
hardcore stuff:

two newlyweds
  holding hands
    on a moonlit beach

breakdown

love,
today i saw two small children
playing in the snow

at first they were rolling around
pulling at each other and laughing

then they were pushing each other
and giggling

then came the shoving and the harsh words

finally came the fists and the crying

anniversary

love is also

standing over
a three-year-old grave
still wishing
there was something you could do

lycanthropy (1967)

perhaps
it was the knapsack
and the long hair

perhaps
it was because
it was an express
and the bus driver
shouldnt have stopped

i don't know...

i just paid my fare and made my way
to the back the best i could

but
it wasnt until after
i seated myself and
pretended i was absorbed
by something out the window

did the occupants return
to their seats

retract their fangs

did the hair on the back
of their necks finally flatten

high school memory

they claw at each other's face
pull out each other's hair
scream—cry as they kick and bite

—in the school yard
two females of the species
engage in rare
physical combat

everyone gathers round
rooting for this one
or that one
but no one dares
break it up
no one dares!
  not the older boys
  not even the nuns

for these two slight Catholic girls
writhing like vicious little ermine
fight with such furor

they don't even care
that their panties show

words

after
a heated argument
this morning
    and having all day
    said nothing
    to one another
tonight
in the same bed
facing
different directions
    both of us
    feigning sleep
i wish
that one of us
would reconcile
that there could be peace
    and silence
    between us again

1st birthday (for Mariette)

trying to make
my little girl laugh
with funny faces

pulling my mouth wide
sticking my tongue out
crossing my eyes
suddenly i notice
how seriously
shes looking at me

and for a moment there
she was a fully grown woman
looking through a window at an idiot
in an insane asylum

consent form

attached to the
Ontario driver's license:

"If you wish to donate your
body or part of your body
for transplant or other
humanitarian purposes, after
death, please complete the
form to the right.
If you do not wish to be
a donor, please detach and
destroy the consent form."

whhewww!
ripped it up just in time!

they almost killed me
off there for a moment!

chipmunk in a wheel

The planet we call Earth
rotates on its axis
at 1,000 mph (at its equator)
every 23 hr 56 min 4.1 sec

The Earth orbits a star
which we call the Sun
at 66,000 mph
every 365.25 days

Both Earth and Sun (and the rest
of the solar system) are reeling towards
the constellation we call Hercules
at 45,000 mph

The solar system belongs to a galaxy
which we call the Milky Way
which is speeding on collision course
towards another galaxy which we call Andromeda
at 1,350,000 mph

This while my pet chipmunk hurries
in his wheel at 12 revolutions per second

Man knows all this
which is why man is going to die

But chipmunks don't know this

Chipmunks have no name
for cage, time and death

Chipmunks know no science
but *are* science

Man is going to die

But a chipmunk in a wheel
is going places

spring (for Fred Cogswell)

little boy birds chasing
little girl birds who try their best to escape
so they can be caught better

abiogenesis

see how it grows?

the plum tree over her grave
glistens in the sun

its limbs stretch
its leaves wax
its blossoms open

its roots draw
from ashes and dust

see how she lives?

in this life, consider and believe:
all theories hold water

love poem

her eyes were not eyes
of lustrous sapphire
but dusty
       like roadside chicory

her hair was not hair
of Egyptian-sun gold
but faded
       like open-field mullein

her hands were not hands
of translucent white quartz
but pallid
       like common Queen Anne's lace

he was a simple country boy
who said to his girl:
I LOVE YOU

this, no man
ever spoke to a woman before

the jungle

the jungle is vast
and i am blind
               stumbling
without reference point

but i am not lost

stranger

i too have been awakened by the thief
have had the glint of steel blind my eye
have heard him shuffle beside my bed
have held my breath
have prayed to god
have seen the knife whole and plunging
have screamed and clawed at
dream's thin air
have awakened into the undream
a murdered man

there is no stranger—
god knows there is no stranger i fear more
than the stranger of myself

aquariums

scientists and common sense
tell us it cannot be done—

for the past two hours
i have been staring in
at my two new kuhli loaches
who insist (writhing their bodies
like little eels and bumping
their noses against the sides)
that they can pass through glass
(and more
that air is water)

—men and their truths standing
so long and staring into their aquariums
should not contradict the theories of fish

peeping tom

i sometimes catch myself
glancing
into lighted rooms
where i see men and women
doing many unexpected things
and sometimes i find myself
staring
into dark windows
straining my eyes to see
and i see many terrible things
like husbands beating their wives
and wives not caring
and murderers lurking behind closet doors
and prostitutes luring young boys
and lovers cheating on their lovers
and i have become
a very nervous person
i am afraid to enter dark rooms
i am afraid to trust myself to sleep
i am afraid because

voyeurs see themselves a lot

some inner light

some inner light
corresponds to that faint little star up there
little star which
exists many years ago
possibly has died
and only light
remains
some reckless god within me
might easily pluck it from the skies
were it there
i am constantly on guard
against him
hesitate to know
the whether of its
existence
so much depends
on its being there

hangover

im sick as a bastard rat

im puking my guts out
over the toilet bowl

my stomach has nothing more
to offer than green bile

every time i heave
i see yellow blotches against
the inside of my eyelids

and just when i think
it cant get any worse
from outside the window
comes the noxious laughter

of little children playing

old question reasked

where do you look for love?

i will tell you how
to find love:

never look for the bird
but look for the camouflage

a beak will appear
then a song

a head—feathers—
feet will shuffle
on a branch

the feathers will ruffle
the bird will flutter
a song will shrill

and the bird will fly
from its absolute space

alight on the shoulders
of your heart

this is when you have found love

replay

watching the Olympics coverage
on television—
a replay of yesterdays
cycling race—
though i know
the inevitable outcome
i find myself
pounding my knees
biting my fists
rooting for
a predetermined loser

freedom

maybe i should have waited
until we were out of the woods

maybe there was another way

maybe i shouldnt have talked to her like that
telling her plain that we were through

maybe i shouldnt have made her cry
made her turn and walk away from me

but what could i do

she turned
and walked away from me

walked away before i was sure

and i
with the new freedom i wanted
watched
as she walked away

walked away and out of sight
while i just stood there

my legs heavy
like the trunks of trees

license to kill

the hunter who just
argued with me that
he has the right to tramp
my land
came *this* close
to blowing my head off

it was in his contorted face
his trigger finger
his profanities

and i know
that if his permit had
Human on it instead
of *Small Game*

i would be a dead duck

haircut, 1969

after all these years
of
    "Why doncha git a haircut
    ya dirty hippy?"
or
    "Lookit the beard. What are those
    creeps tryna prove anyway?"
today
i walk down the street
with my beard shaved off
my hair cut short
and feel like an idiot

feel like a damn exhibitionist

out of reach

watching her
seeing her
so beautifully
sleeping beside me like that—

sometimes
it's the thing already possessed
one covets the most

anxiety attack

i am awakened
jump up
slap
my face
throw
water on
my head
take
two tran
quilizers
climb
back
into bed
knowing
there is
nothing
to be afraid of

and being afraid of it

newspaper item

It was reported this morning
that a man
attempting to cross the St Joseph Blvd
was struck by a car and knocked to the pavement
while the car sped away.
The man, recovering his feet,
was immediately hit by a second onrushing car
which also hurled on.
Regaining his feet,
he was knocked down by yet a third car
which also sped away without stopping.
Half conscious, the unidentified man
barely managed in reaching the shoulder of the blvd
when a fourth car, running him over,
and killing him, hastened on
towards its destination.

natural selection/flowers over a grave

for a day, these ephemerals;
for a year, annuals;
for two, biennials;
for several, perennials...

each dying that the other may live

and somewhere beyond
the body's genealogies;
the mind's philosophies;
the heart's dreams;
the poet's poems...

the soul too must change its way

i have learned little in this life of
what there is to know, the summation
of which is this truth:
all flowers become eternals; for nothing living
(the body, the heart, the mind,
the soul) dies—only constantly is
reborn

over and over again

trespass (for Ernest Buckler)

there was a sudden rap on my door
  a friend perhaps
    and i am too late to turn the lock

for my nerves are bad
  and i am overtired
    and don't want to talk to anyone

so like a criminal in my own home
  i take refuge in the bathroom
    hide behind the half-closed door

my friend knocks louder
  opens the door
    yells my name into my house

i am shaking all over
  terrified he'll come in
    and for some reason check the bathroom

and there he'll find me—cringing
  caught in an act of committing a crime
    far more heinous
than his trespass could ever be

the girl with the radio

ive come to the beach for fun
but havent found it yet

the suns too hot
the waters too cold
the kids are too loud

im not happy
and im not unhappy

i don't know what the matter is

i don't want to go home
and i don't want to stay
and the girl with the radio on
changed the station—the bitch

the poet's lot

i remember going
with this girl
for the longest time
was even engaged
to be married to her
whose parents were
continuously trying
to break us up
because
being a poet
there was something
"funny" about me
"obviously a fag"

conquest

he wanted a conquest
he wanted to be renowned
he said: i shall swim
to that island
his friends laughed
mocking him
but by god he did it
he dragged himself
from the waters
he was overcome with joy
he jumped up and down
waving at the distant
onlookers
but already they had turned away
for though they knew
that none among them could
achieve the same

the island was but an island

discovery

in the
bus station
because
i am
normal
feel
justified
in staring
at the
crippled
retard
who
suddenly
he sees
me seeing
him
advances
sits
beside me
gawks
i get up
limp
horribly
into
the washroom
where
for the next
two hours

make faces
at myself
in the
mirror

:beware the idiot
he is you,
me

perception

then there was
the man who after
99 years opened his door
to night, who

now possesses nothing
but the memory of that moment
the glimpse of darkness blinded him

folie du doute

late at night
  nothing to do
nowhere to go
wandering the deserted streets
of an unknown city
  i am being
  followed by a dog

casually
i round a corner
  back
  suddenly flat
  against brick
the dog unsuspectingly...

HHYYAAA! GIT OUTTA HERE
YOU STUPID GODDAMN DOG!

and the dog yelps
runs down the street
disappears into the distance
  going godknowswhere now
  to do godknowswhat

and i...
wandering the deserted streets
of an unknown city

wonder
  if perhaps...
                perhaps i should follow him

dog days

nothing moving
nothing happening at all
and i couldnt care less

no one worth talking to
nothing worth reading
nothing worth listening to

just sitting here
on the edge of a railway bridge
my legs wondering
whether to dangle or swing

Susan,

my love for you
is a bird

a bird of love
which is my heart

he sings his song
of love for you
but you cannot hear him
because of his cage

i will take my heart
from my breast
gift it to you

take it home
sleep with it
hold it to *your* breast

and if he does not sing for you
then let him fly freely
for i will never need
my heart again

it will be enough to know
you held it to your breast

it will be enough to know
somewhere his small wings
are beating in the distance

mask

saw the Beatles—
they had a message...
man, i beat those drums
till the crowd yelled
"More, Ringo, More!"

but just before
the lights went on
i slipped off stage
camouflaging myself
as one of the crowd

moral words

i get very angry
when people tell me what
i *should* or *shouldnt* do

people should realize that
"should" is a moral word

people shouldnt tell other people
what they *should* and *shouldnt* do

on the morning of my execution

and dont try anything funny, sonny
the hangman threatened

as he tightened
the noose about my neck

the hole he dug

a man was obsessed
by a nugget of gold

furiously he dug
with the strength of a thousand

finally exhausted
he fell to his knees

"Now if only a ladder
to reach the ore!" he cried

10-minute porn flick

i saw it i tell you!
just at the very end

a couple having performed
for the camera
with precise professionalism
and closeup detail
every kind of sex act possible—

i saw it!:
        just for a flashing moment
        a brief glimpse
        of human acknowledgment
        a meeting of eyes

a split second
of true romantic love

fantasies

in a small dingy room
  of a small dingy brothel
    of the red-light district
an unhappily married
  business man has his
    fetishes actualized
as the aging prostitute
  dreams one step closer to
    her fenced suburban detached

complete with husband and kids

arachneophobia

a spider lives
in a hole
where my tub
adjoins
the bathroom wall

his omnipresence
has really got to me
his hairy little existence
must be terminated

somehow
i must call upon
all my courage
muster together
all my strengths

ignore him

Saviour

in the beginning they had Fear
  therefore a need
    then came the man

the man suited their needs
  discarded their fears
    and they hailed him a Saviour

the Saviour died
  but the need went on
    therefore Words

the Words spoke of him as God
  so they built houses
    on the foundation of their Book

and down through the ages
  they gathered there
    in their Houses of Words

and their mouths worshipped him

people i know

last night i dreamed
of a schoolmate who sat
at the back of the class in grade five

that was thirty years ago
and i have never thought of him since

he was neither friend nor adversary

i neither liked him
nor disliked him
yet
know his name now
and see his face
as clearly as then

and what of all the others:
hundreds
even thousands—
people i knew
only for hours
             minutes
                  seconds
  a doorman at a hotel
  a waiter at a pub
  a pretty girl who got off a bus
  a receptionist in an office

their faces as vivid
as my own in a mirror
all of them a part of me
through memory

and why should it be so important tonight
as i sit here alone on the edge of my bed
that i cant stop thinking of them—

cant stop wondering
if any of them
ever wonder about me

Earl Flynn

i remember Earl Flynn
who
because he wouldnt like guns
and couldnt stand pain
was dared by the boys
to pull the trigger
and graze the mane
and who later
cried as he stumbled
gun in hand through
dark woods in rain
just wanting to put
the poor animal
out of its misery

suspicion (for Ed)

the grouse were thin
and the walk long
with our heavy guns
we hunted the spruce
i in front of him
looking back
sometimes
at the barrel of his twenty gauge
and he is my friend
and i know it
and i know
that he is no madman

photographs of myself

there are many hundreds of photographs
  and sometimes i sit for hours
    trying to *realize*
them—some gesture
  which might remind
    me of me
but all of these people are dead—
  all of them and perhaps
    they had never lived
and each time i wonder
  Who...Why...until...
    then a pattern forms

and someone within me dies again

poem

since all things
  exist only
    within their opposites
do not tell me i am determined.
  do not say to me
    i am addicted
to drink, dope and wicked women;
  lo!
    i have found freedom
linked to the end of the chain

10,000 years
(words over recent grave)

when was it you died now?
when was it your ashes buried?

  when do i stop counting the months?

what do i remember as good times?
what do i remember as bad times?

  when did the memories start choosing me?

when do i stop talking to you?
when do you stop talking to me?

  i think we're in trouble, Franny

:already fossils
               are forming
                            in the strata

nightchoir on Smith's Lake

    from
    the lake's fringes
           and beyond
songs
      of herons
          bitterns
               frogs
and
      as i suddenly stood there

QUIET!

and
      i could not even hear
memory
         as the echo of sound

and then
        as gradually
            as *déjà vu*
i became aware of
and was absorbed
          in the
             antiphony

the *real*
      silence there
the CLAMOUR
        of the
           human listening

Dog,

i hate you

i hate you
and your kind

you are the scum
of the zoological world

i hate you more today
than i did yesterday

you are too eager
for the food
i owe you for your service

i will make you wait
another hour

i hate you
for your expectancy

i hate you
for your obviousness

i hate you
for not hating me back

i hate you
for wagging your tail
when i finally
bring you your meal

but most of all
i hate you for this
miserable leash
you have me tethered to

a matter of substantial importance

DAMN!

just remembered
a pair of dirty shorts
beside the bed...
gotta get up...
no matter how tired...
gotta stash them someplace...
dont wanna die in my sleep...
have them found there...
gotta get up...
cant...
too tired...
gotta sleep...

he is awakened in the middle of the night

though i know
it could only be you
who moves through
the rooms darkness
i cannot see to verify
and in quick
hesitant
voice
beseech you answer me:
"Is that you darling?
Is that you?"

whiteout

here
with everything ive always wanted
EVERY THING a man could ask for
i am struck suddenly
by the sickgut feeling
that nothing has been accomplished
that there is no continuation
and in looking backwards
that i have left no footprints

hippy (1970)

when i showed up at his door
15 years later
he didnt know me

he didnt *want* to know me

he had no *time* for me

he couldnt recall
a single moment
of the 10 years
we spent as kids together

he *had* to get back to work

and as he drove away
i watched his frown relax
in the review mirror
as i grew smaller and smaller

until he had no *space* for me

there

in the
middle
of my
cedar bush
one mile
back
alone and
hurt
from a
stupid accident
for a moment
i lay
in pain
gawking
about me
lest
somebody
saw

red giant—white dwarf

lying
on my back
at the beach
squinting
at the sun
thinking
5 billion years from now...

me
26 years old
with a life expectancy
of 78
suddenly
really
PARANOID OVER IT

evolution

men who stand on
cliffs
longing for avian flight
might do better to
consider
their evolutionary lot:

during the Triassic
we nearly *became*
the birds
but luckily evolved
as terrestrials
who now can envy
what the birds know not

thanatophobia

i was today informed by my psychologist
that i have been suffering from a neurotic disorder:
the abnormal fear of death

i have pledged the remainder of my days
to the pursuit of acquiring
that normal degree
one requires

true measure

a man cornered a mouse

the mouse reared
leapt and gnashed at the man

the man stood aback

it takes a mouse to measure a man
it takes a man to measure a mouse

root cellar

as i stood there
behind her
i knew that she knew...

filling her cellar with
carrots...
turnips...
arse...

Jump!

A girl on the 19th story is
standing on a ledge ready to jump.

I am among a crowd who is
shouting "Don't jump!
Don't jump!"

I am shouting "Jump!
Yes, jump! There is
nothing to live for!"

Some uniformed official
grips my shoulder
with his great hairy hand:

"Come with me, sonny.
You're next."

polarization

lost
in the great cedar swamp
i must somehow
keep that North Star
in sight

but its light
disappears
and reappears
then disappears again
my vision blurred by tears
strained eyes blind
to the one true direction
i blundered around in that swamp
for years

the circles ceased
only when i learned to cast my eyes aside
in order to keep the view in sight

and so it is with any purpose:

in seeking the goal
one must not look *too* at it

acrophobia

im terrified of heights
especially tall buildings

don't tell me about
guardrails and glass
—im not afraid of falling
but jumping

even more frightening
is the realization that
im not suicidal

im afraid of jumping
just for the fun of it

night fears

warm room. quiet room.
then what are these thoughts
that now plague my brain?

were days—alone i slept
beneath the stars
a puny fire to keep me sane
from any cat or wolf or bear
that should venture from the wood
to find me sleeping there;
and should the fire dwindle down
from lack of fuel or downpour rain
i was too tired or cold to move
to build the embers up to flame

O that i were a boy!
and able to sleep like that again

Love,

i hold you to my heart
like a home

but how do i tell you this
—you who say
you have never loved—

and how can one
who has never loved
feel how it feels to be spurned

:my heart is an empty house
haunted by something that never
lived there

and never died

for Franny

this:
that love is not two circles
which either
intersect
forming a common denominator
or
which are congruent;
that is to say
there is nothing cofunctional here

but this:
that it is the one thing which is
nondivisible
and yet
is conceived by two parts;
that is to say
two entities which occupy the same space

or in answer your question
will i always love you, this:
we are more than the whole
and the parts can only separate together

nervous breakdown (Foymount, 1971)

by listening to the *too* quiet
i became insane
lying under blankets
i imagined wolverines
with human hands
picking the lock
on my cabin door
so noiselessly they worked
i could not hear them
for the silence
until suddenly
from behind the walls
from within the ceilings
armies
       of mice
           footsteps
                 ceased
each sound was death for me then

every silence an opera

after coon hunting

i don't know about death itself
but
the realization
that the time has come
must be a little like
a treed coon:

two red eyes
staring dumbly
into a blinding
white
light

the man with the knife

in this night
in this strange hotel room
i swear i hear a noise
there is somebody here

THERE IS SOMEBODY IN THIS ROOM WITH ME!

my mind screams fear
my body hesitates to strike the match
maybe it's a monster
or the man with the knife
i know it's the man with the knife

THE MAN WITH THE KNIFE IS IN THIS ROOM WITH ME!

my mind screams fear
my body hesitates to strike the match
in case its true

Werewolves

A werewolf accosted me
on a busy street

"This town has strange people
in it," he whispered

"Not everyone can be as
normal as you and me,"
I answered

and walked on

squirrels

an old man in the park is crying
as he runs about
trying to swat squirrels
with a newspaper
and the squirrels
are making a sport of it
coming so close
then scampering away
and nobody knows
why he hates the squirrels

now if he were an old man
chasing old dreams...
or if he were a young man
chasing young dreams...
but he is an old man
chasing squirrels

and thats the reason for the crying

night

and no far off light.
i am on the road walking
neither away from
or towards.
even sound
is in conspiracy
against me
some misplaced nostalgia
with the absence of dogs
barking in the distance.
enveloped
by the deepest silence
ever
i am on the road walking
listening for...
and hearing
nothing
but an only cricket
here
     or there
busying himself

creating silence

dry spell

what happens
when all the poems are gone
really gone
a drought which
unlike the others
just wont end

if suddenly
i were emptied
with no more poems for people
or myself
or just for their own sake

and when even this poem's trick
wont work anymore

what then?

shoulders

winter. God is in his garden
pulling weeds in the snow
what God knows
is how the winter roses grow

i am among the cedar hedges
God does not see me
is working hard
God had broad shoulders

i am among the snowladen boughs
of cedar trees that grow around
the edge of God's garden
the roses are frozen
rattle
in a glass wind
God does not hear me

i am sneaking up on God
who is stooped over his winter roses
my feet are frozen

God turns to his house
snow falls from my blazer
God has high shoulders
leaves footprints

observation

never heard
    of a theist on
        his deathbed
who suddenly
    *dis*believed
        in God

upon hearing of your death (for Alden Nowlan)

old friend, what a fine pair
of thanatophobes we made:

the countless dark nights
drunk on home brew or chokecherry wine
issuing challenges at
Mr Death himself from
your back veranda

HOW WE WANTED TO PUNCH HIS EYES OUT

and then back
in the more philosophical light
of your kitchen
trying to imagine what
its *really* like until—
like true romantics—
the sudden sobering conclusion
that we really *were* immortal after all

today i was informed of your death

and if i were to believe this—
if i were really to believe this
what a terrible terrible thing i would become

like a blind man afraid of the dark

murderer

on lake Lorwell
my friend and i
fishing in friendship
and the lake is deep
and i know that i am no murderer
but i think
that if i should push him over
he would drown

Tina,

each time i think of you
you plant another tree

   (why do you taunt me
   with such cryptic letters

   why do you not reveal yourself?)

i lie awake thinking of you
all nights

you have made me lonely
and loneliness i think is some
terrible species of the love family

Tina,

i think i am lost
among your terrible trees

and in calling out your name
i hear only the forests of my own heart
being hacked into a clearing

the Vocal Argument

a hermit who was an atheist
lived miles from anywhere

one night a devil came upon him
and beat the atheist to death

now this is the strange part:
the whole while, the man screamed

on the Carlingwood bus

i
happened to glance down
noticed
my fly open
knew
others saw it
too
immediately
looked out
the window
pretended
i saw nothing
rode
all the way
down to
Confederation Square
with
a draft between
my legs
because
that was not
nearly as bad
as having them
see that
i knew they knew

mistaken identity

i thought i
recognized her
sitting in the shade
of a tall elm tree

   (she always loved
   the elm trees)

i ran towards her
calling her name
for the first time
in fifteen years

   MARLENE! MARLENE!
   IS THAT YOU MARLENE!?

but it wasn't Marlene

: what is it they say
about the roots
and the branches of trees...

poem

she had nothing to say to me

i had nothing to say to her

see how all words
eventually become poems?

the comedian

tonight i have been
made to realize
i am not a person
to be taken seriously

tonight close friends
thrash through
my latest manuscripts with

  you gotta read this one, John!

  ha ha! that's a good one, Bernie!

  youre something else, man!

laughing over
what i consider to be
the most poignant and serious
love and death poems
ive ever written

the floor monster

its late
in bed my right arm dangles
                                over
its hand touches the floor

suddenly
        the realization
that something actually *could*
live under there

of course its ridiculous
i know that

but it has teeth
and lives on the flesh and blood
off live hands

the favour

the wind blew the seed
beside a hunk of granite

"Come closer" said the stone
"for I hold the moisture that you may grow"

the seed grew
and grew from a sapling into a towering tree

one day the granite spoke
"Friend, I need a favour"

"Not today" said the tree
"I have a headache"

"Yes today" said the stone
"for you owe me one"

"I OWE YOU NOTHING!" bellowed the tree
and flexing his roots he broke the granite

but the stone was two stones

murder confession

she shouldn't have been
hitchhiking along
a dark road like that
    miniskirt
    see-through blouse
O the fire that raged inside
as i tore the clothes away
and everything was fine
until she started to scream...

theres not much else you *can* do but kill them
when they scream like that you know...

The eagle & the mountain

An eagle looked down from his mountaintop
and noticed a mouse on a big rock

"Hey Mouse! Would you like me to fly you up here
where you can see the world from a mountaintop?"
asked the eagle

"Thanks eagle, but I'm already on a mountaintop,"
answered the mouse

strangers (unexpected meeting)

why is the distance
so strange
between us
was it not

expected?

we are not
strangers

only exlovers

why
do we not shatter
this uneasy silence
with words to one another?

enemies
would do more
sitting across from one another

why?

: the silence is All
and is interrupted
only by a deeper
more

distant

    silence

dog days

sitting
on a park bench
staring out
over the stagnant
water

a little boy
on a tricycle
rides up
singing
      "Diddle diddle dum
      diddle diddle dee—
      whatcha doin' mister?"

"NOTHIN' LITTLE BOY"

      "whatcha lookin' at mister?"

"NOTHIN' LITTLE BOY"

      "Whatcha havin' for lunch mister"

"NOTHIN' LITTLE BOY"

      "I'm havin' hot dogs—
      bye mister"

and away he rides
on his tricycle
until out of sight

and me
sitting on a park bench
staring out over the water
singing

"DIDDLE DIDDLE DUM
DIDDLE DIDDLE DEE"

Old movie

The beautiful runaway Anne Baxter is a famished pickpocket who gets caught in the act by a handsome carnival barker who gives her a job washing dishes at the carnival although he's a playboy cad who just wants her for her body but the big ugly mute carnival strongman freak who sees her *really* falls in love with her and the handsome highdiver who makes Anne his assistant falls in love with her as well and asks her to marry him and at a carnival party she breaks the news and even the big ugly mute carnival strongman freak gives Anne a little peck on the neck and is happy for her and the diver's handsome photographer friend takes promotional pictures of them and makes them famous and later the cad wants money from Anne that he loaned her in the beginning and he hits Anne but she kisses him passionately despite of it and her husband catches them and a fistfight occurs and the diver beats the cad up and tells the owner to kick him out of the show as the big ugly mute carnival strongman freak looks on and the diver tells Anne they're leaving the show also but Anne won't go because she's basically a tramp and is still in love with the cad but then she makes up with her husband and the next day he is killed by a fall from the dive ladder and the photographer comforts Anne and after the funeral the nice carnival owner shows Anne where her husband kept his money and the will he left gives it all to Anne and she stays with the carnival but the cad comes sleazing back and Anne sleeps with him but when she wakes up all her money is gone and Anne turns tough and demands more money from the owner for diving but she is injured in the dive pool and they take her to the hospital while the carnival packs up and moves to another city and the photographer falls in love with Anne too and wants to marry her and Anne is confused and doesn't know if she loves *him* or the cad so goes back to the carnival and the big ugly mute carnival strongman freak brings her some flowers and Anne is touched and thanks him and he goes away and then the cad shows up and comes back to Anne's tent after the show and kisses her but his magic doesn't work anymore and she calls him filth

and he strikes her again and tells him to get out and he admits that
he killed her husband and he tries to strangle her but the big ugly
mute carnival strongman freak throws him off her and chases him
up the Ferris wheel and the freak climbs up to the top too and
grabs hold of the cad and throws him down to the ground dead and
Anne beckons him down by telling him that the police won't hurt
him and the big ugly mute carnival strongman freak comes down
from the Ferris wheel and the police take him away as Anne looks
on

"Poor Bernell," she says

God

i knocked on God's door
but nobody was home

i tried peeking through the windows
but the shades were drawn

i tried opening the door
but it was locked

—bolted shut from the inside

§§§

BOOKS

I can really draw eagles (1970), *seeds we planted* (1972), *)parentheses(* (1974) *the theories of fish* (1979), *in my own image* (1984), *dog days* (1994), *birds of passage* (1996), *abiogeneses* (1999), *The Monster of Moneymore* (2004), *One Day the Animals Talked* (2005), *Zoopoesies* (2009), *poems in f minor* (2014), *The Moneymorians* (2014), *Wine River* (2016), *Gypsy* (2016), *The Black Wolf* (2018), *Collected Stories* (2018), *An Illustrated Miscellany of Animal Facts, Feats & Records* (2019), *Out of Kilter* (2020)

PERIODICALS and ANTHOLOGIES

Abbey, Aberdeen University Review (Scotland), *The Alchemist, Aldebaran, Amber, And Having Writ, The Antigonish Review, Arrows* (England), *Art:mag, Aspect, The Atlantic Advocate, Bardic Echoes, The Black Bear Review, Blackberry, The Brunswickan, Canada Goose, Canadian Author & Bookman and Canadian Poetry, Cave* (New Zealand), *CBC Alarm Clock* (radio broadcast), *CBC Anthology* (radio broadcast), *Circus Maximus, The Communicator, Copperfield, Cyclo Flame, The Dekalb Literary Arts Journal, East River Review, Echoes of the Unlocked Odyssey, El Viento, Encore!, Encore! Encore!, Etc: a Review of General Semantics, Eureka* (Sweden), *Event, Experiment, The Fiddlehead, Floorboards, The Gaspereau Review, Global Tapestry Review, Gone Soft, Hi-time, Huerfano, Inky Trails, Inlet, Intercourse, The Islander, Jam To-day, Jean's Journal of Poems, The Lake Superior Review, The Lark and the Sky, Linq, Lion's Head Magazine, Madrona, Mamashee, Mati, Microkosmos, Minotaur, Mississippi Review, The Mountain Thought Review, Nimrod, Northeast Journal,*

Northern Light, Origins, Other Voices, Outrigger (New Zealand), *Panachee, Pegasus* (BC), *Pegasus* (Nevada), *Penny Dreadful, Phoebe, Poetry Nippon* (Japan), *The Poets of Prince Edward Island, Poets of '74, The Pottersfield Portfolio, Portals, Remembrance, Rosewood Review, Salt, Scroll, Serendipity, Sinter* (Switzerland), *South & West, Southern Review* (Australia), *Speak 2, Speak Out, Streaks of Light, Sunburst #9, Sunburst #10, Sunday Clothes, Talisman, These are my Jewels, Tide, Twigs, Two Tone* (Rhodesia), *Unicorn Reader, Valhalla, Weid: the Sensibility Review, The Windless Orchard, Windows, Writer's Exchange*

Made in the USA
Monee, IL
28 February 2020